It's World That Makes The Love Go Round

modern poetry
selected from
BREAKTHRU International
Poetry Magazine

Also published by Corgi Books

LOVE LOVE LOVE

The New Love Poetry
Edited by Pete Roche

It's World That Makes The Love Go Round

Modern Poetry
Selected from
BREAKTHRU International Poetry Magazine

Edited with an Introduction
by
KEN GEERING

IT'S WORLD THAT MAKES THE LOVE GO ROUND

A CORGI BOOK 552 08053 5

Poems from
BREAKTHRU International Poetry Magazine,
Editor: Ken Geering,
38 Penn Crescent,
Haywards Heath,
Sussex, England.

Printing History
Corgi Edition published 1968

Acknowledgements: page 124

This book is set in Bembo 11 pt.

Corgi Books are published by Transworld Publishers, Ltd.,
Bashley Road, London, N.W.10

Made and printed in Great Britain by
Richard Clay (The Chaucer Press), Ltd., Bungay, Suffolk

INTRODUCTION.

Eight years ago we put out our first issue of Breakthru. The seeds of today's bi-monthly 'pantechnicon of verse' were sown.

A prominent Little Magazine editor—who's not around these days—is reputed to have said: 'I'll give it six months!' Another felt that it was Ken Geering who should have been given six months. Be that as it may, many hundreds of poets have come into poetry via our (often smugly condemned) press advertisements. Including some who are now internationally known.

We present 120 Breakthru poets, confident that their meaningful, often racy, gnomic, aphoristic poetry will attract readers who are sated with 'formalistic', gimmicky verse; or with dull, stylistically imitative 'trad' work—to which the gimmicky verse is a legitimate but exaggerated reaction.

We have consciously, deliberately—and predictably—erred on the side of 'mass assault'. We hope that readers will accept our decision *not* to provide a 'representative selection' from a smaller number of poets, but to build up general themes, illustrated with a succession of many fresh, new, different-styles poems which maintain *interest* at a high level. Even at the price of the mildly staccato effect which results from any quickly moving chiaroscuro of poets and styles.

Section headings introduce loosely assembled, like-theme poems. Where content clashes with form, we sometimes—unforgivably—come down on the side of content. Occasionally, form is the reason for an inclusion. Almost always, however, we have tried to include poems which weld content to good poetry form—*whole* poems. Form without content is mere tinsel, and content minus form is prose, masquerading.

Many of our poets are very young. Some will be known. Some almost unknown. A fair number are unknown for inexcusable reasons bound up with the mechanics of Britain's uneven poetry scene.

We believe that this is a good, *live*, honest—at times exciting—collection. We thank our poets and our readers for *participating* in our poetry: which is in love with *life*.

KEN GEERING.

LIST OF SECTIONS

HUMOUR

and I could laugh; dying; the smallest section: because, said Brecht: 'he who laughs has not yet heard the fearful news . . .'

Dead Beat — David J. Lee

I'm lying in bed one day,
And this jerk
With tubes in his ears
Sticks something cold on my chest,
And says something I can't hear.

It must be important,
Because soon people are washing me,
Like I got lice.
But I don't mind,
I'm too idle to wash myself.

And I say nothing
When my folks arrive,
And make with the tears.

But then they put me in this box:
It's comfortable,
But not exactly spacious.
And when they bang the lid on,
I'm worried, and I yell:
'Open the box'
But I can't,
And this guy upstairs says:
'How do you like the mystery prize?'
And I don't.

Timid in the Rain

Malcolm Woolridge

Cold dripping rain
Battered the bones of my head

Pummelled my skull
Squeezing sharp tears
Raining rivulets
From my sousled scalp.
Cringing into the concrete post
Huddling sheepish
From the driving sopping cold.
Shivering, with tarry traffic
Slurping squelching by.
I dared not ask her,
Look for her, wait for her
Accepting rebuff
In soaking soggy sloshy cold.
My love has a brolly
And warmth in her eye—
But I am too timid
And let things pass by.

Arms and Armour

Ernest Ed Arps

'Looking for courage in a jug of beer?
Tell me, my love, what dragon do
    you fear?'
'Darling, my terror is of you, no less,
Armed to the teeth with tea and
    righteousness'.

⁑ *Man* ⁑ *in* ⁑ *Orbit* ⁑

D. O. Pitches

* * * * * *
* While * freighting * f
rom * Earth * to * Venus * we
* passed * a * man * without * a *
spacesuit. * He * was * not * pleasant
* to * look * at, * orbiting * the * Sun.
* And * I * remembered * how * he * w
ould * repeat * a * modish * phrase * ba
ck * on * Earth, * endlessly- * Stop *
the * world, * I * want * to * get
* off. * And * it * appeared * t
hat * someone * had. *
* * * * * *

Dear God

D. W. K. Cotton

dEar god
plrase ecscuse mY
wriTeing to yow wen
you don evern nO me
an Pleese doN t½? tHin
me rOod fow saYin iT
But i thIngk sumwUn
uP theyre haS maid
Asmal mIsstak
You se iam gEtin@g
too OR thRe otther
peples baDD luk
ass weLlasmI
Own
10tso ff lovE
deNNis;

For Samuel B . . . . . . D. O. Pitches

Estragon, Vladimir, Pozzo, and Lucky
Were looking the other way,
When Godot Came
Stood there Unnoticed
And Decided not to stay.

A Brief Analysis of the Darwin Theory Richard Catesby

A Chair has four legs
Man has two
If he had any more
He'd be in a zoo.

Free Gift? Gerald England

I got some tissues with my coffee yesterday,
And last week I got a lady's handkerchief!
Instant coffee—
Is that what causes my colds?

Hand Out the Song Sheets, Dora's Climbed Another Mountain David Kernek

Dora, Dora
  female explorer
    whose Left Thigh
      continually gains the admiration of
        the Himalayan
          Foothills
            —'tis of thee I dream

Dora, Dora
  unchain your Mosquito Net
    lay down your map
      my navigation knows no bounds

Dora, Dora
  please become a Social Worker
    father nightly wets the bed
      he is starved nightly
        of my Understanding and the
          ultimate realisation of
            his fantasies

Dora, Dora
  female explorer
    of not inconsiderable fame
      did you really wear leather
        knickers
          in the Upper Reaches of
            the Amazon?

Dora, Dora
female explorer
you are climbed
because
you are there

'Petronella' Jeffrey Grenfell-Hill

'Petronella darling don't play down there,
Come and have tea with Auntie and me,
It's nice and sunny here on the lawn
And there's lots of strawberry jam.
We'll even let you pick the currants
And leave the rest of the scone.
Petra, please, don't kick the cat,
And do stop picking your nose.

Yes, she's seven this year
And so affectionate too.
Don't throw stones at Mummy dear,
They might go in her eyes.
Auntie has brought you a present
My love, come, kiss her and say
Hullo—Petra! No, I think the little
Dear said 'Oh! well.'

Petra don't dig up the dahlias,
And do give your knickers a tug.
I don't like you playing down there
My love, the goblins will catch
You I'm sure—you'll kill them!
Well, come and have tea with Auntie and me,
And we'll let you drink out of the saucer,
It's one of her off days you know.

Petronella! You've now gone too far,
You've covered the table with sod,
I know you don't care, but Auntie
Is here, and she loves little girls like you.
Leave the dahlias alone,
No, we don't want a hole,
And do stop screaming down there—
Oh! dear, she's found Uncle George . . .'

Aynshunt Ayelind.
Summer 1965

Michael F. Golding

Twisted reveries on white fibre spilled
tortuous pain quarterized by h s morbidly
first, then
luvlyfe wiv j harthrugg soxov
awl songs to disenchant, butt
cawl the sayveyur ov our soles
poit ov this strayned new werld
o sayve noo inglind ailing jinsbeard
strayte tawk those bumb crayzed polifliks
bi yor bist for litter werds ewsing!
yew wont gitt nikkd, thunk lady c.
showt for help for yew hav frends
awl wiv it now und vury mowdem mit
de lungwige ere cums lorinse feelinsherty
awl hayl undoo ris cela salgoud emoh
und is mayts wiv awl the pekkoonery gott
mit de scul wottery? rong blowk, ees bin dun
then arfter harried wilstrip evrywun
ees gott hoogmince prublimbs wott wiv
redisha und le prinsly fingry inn,
de fonunce bull und awl fat crab,
vootnumb herting evry day butt no wun
helps por harried ceptic sob rillion
und bown dyaz hoo make evry boddy sud
wid der singeing und thay then boo por
wilstrip lowder. lewkout ere cums
hairgory caustic wiv iss mad yaks . . .

Ebb Tide

Margo Laird

At the back of our hotel were the miles of dunes,
Sand dunes, and midnight sky,
And the rising moon.
And you, my love, were there.

At the front of our hotel were the sea and the sand,
The sound of the sea was a sigh,
And the sand was washed by the moon,
And you, O! My love, were there.

When the morning came for departing,
And the taxi man honked at the door,
The sand was warm to the hand on the dunes,
And warm underfoot on the shore . . .
But you were not there any more.
You were still in the sea where I pushed you,
Where I wish I had pushed you before.

More War Memoirs

Ernest Ed Arps

I've never made the claim to be
The means of speeding victory,
Indeed my poor old colonel reckons
I delayed it several seconds.

LOVE—

we'll invest in love-mines and hope they're open-cast . . . and HATE, out of which is love born often . . .

Marvels — Everard Flintoff

I've seen comets magnetised athwart the spires
Of Oxford, The Brocken Spectre with tyres
Of colour around its head. I have memorized

The voc-abulary of volcanoes in
Iceland, seen three moons at once near Oxenhope,
Started at a moon rainbow's tin

Glint above Leeds City Station, but that weird
Heart-shaped sun I saw between clouds at Rossall,
Whiteness all around it, like some colossal

Ace in the hand of that dummy, Nature,
Has only been trumped once, when you, you
    clever creature,
Played your almond eyes and won an
    aging teacher.

Poem Asoka Weerasinghe

O lotus face,
I want to make patterns
upon your breasts;
brush your masses
of gilded hair,
and bind them with
a perfumed festoon
of spring flowers.
Place many bracelets
studded with gems
upon your hands,
and watch those pink
lips quiver after
a bath of kisses,
and whisper secrets
into your grey eyes.

Dedicated to the Rather Attractive Girl who Works at The Hairdresser's on the Hill. Titled: In Event of Emergency, Call Me. Malcolm F. Cox

'Excuse me madam, your eyes are on fire!'

Miss Pike and Miss Minnow Juanita Peirse

Miss Pike loves God in a wholesome way;
From her corner seat in the second pew
Where two or three are gathered to pray
Miss Pike will render to God His due.

Whether erring and straying or being forgiven,
Miss Pike's emotions are neat and tidy:
Christened, confirmed, confessed and shriven,
She can smile for Christmas and weep on Good Friday.

Miss Pike gives most careful thought to others,
Sends all her old clothes to the Jumble Sale.
She will always chat to the married mothers
And never jumps over the altar rail.

Miss Minnow's love is a different story.
'Minnow', said God, 'why hurtest thou me?'
And her heart was rent with the power and the glory,
And her side with the pains of Calvary.

She gave up her wealth as though for a lark,
She tended the dying and nourished the sick;
She witnessed her Lord from a tub in Hyde Park,
They called her a harmless lunatic.

But her relatives simply refused to agree,
And no doubt it was shocking and rather silly—
When she asked the Bishop to sit at tea
Next an elderly harlot from Piccadilly.

While Miss Pike is redeemed by a decorous sip
From a murmuring priest with a ritual cup,
Christ presses His wounds to Miss Minnow's lip,
So she doesn't notice they've locked her up.

Memo to a Town Planner — Richard Herbert

'. . . and sometimes
in these very streets
the Hitler Youth
would take it
into their heads
to march . . .

. . . and when we heard
their trumpets
and their drums
then we would all
without exception
seek refuge
in the nearest house . . .

. . . In those days
you understand
the doors
would always open . . .'

An Offer — R. L. Parsley

There are many places
I've never been
She
Is one of them.
There are many things
I've never seen
Who
Wants to travel?

2 Up Left Ann Thomson

with the first betrayal
the precedent was set
now you pass your
days by the window,
incredulous,
like some hunger-eyed
madonna
waiting to be rediscovered
and your arms ache
from the emptiness
and sometimes
the whole street rocks
with the cries
of your hands.

Silhouette Girl David John Staniland

Silhouette girl in a plastic mac
Standing here beside the green rolling sea.
Give me your hand little outlined girl,
And I will guide you to the
Tender landscape of my heart's love.
Once there we may stroll away
And reach the rainbow's end.
Come touch the stars:
Can't you see?
They twinkle, as do the diamonds
Whispering in your eyes.

For Sweet-Dee

Michael Parker

i drifted around for
the year and day   but folding
that mem oreal
times, i
drifted.

sweet dee alove warm
leers around my
mind drifting
as i.

hair black trace
is tickle in
my mind.

so i drifted around
    the time
i spend
            drifting.

always around i am
all ways around my mind,
hers ter
feel a pain.

but no ease-he-lies
to say he lies,

ease-he-come
                    and ease-he-go.

too young to no
                        i fear

i say humm
bleed, in me
    her knows in
need of he.

i drifted around for
the yearn of a day   but
forlorn leaves
hold my drift
around my
                    years.

The Western World — John Blyth

O that dear girl
and the swirl of thc sky-washed sea
where we sat at the turn of the long tide,
and love that could ride those breaker
foaming windspent glances—
O the dance of enchanted eyes!—
till the cry of abandoned gull;
skull beneath soft hair;
time's lament for an unheard air,
drove our hearts to deception.
Perception of cheating time
should not leave such lime-set webs
that our beds lie barren,
and the fields of time yield dry thorns.
Yet there yawns this gulf of confusion
in each recognizing glance,
while the dances of love (as on swords)
present this only beauty of the western world.

Dreams Peter J. Whitehead

I lost you in the intricate web
  Of my imagination, in the words and gestures
Which I wove around your name.
  And I created another and more tractable you
Who satisfied the less the more I forced her to comply.
  Until at last, stripping aside all artifacts, I met—
Myself, coming the other way. 'Is she still with you?'
  I ventured. The reply was fierce.
'Yes, you feel. Do you imagine I would lose the track?
  Dreams are the pattern stitched across the cloth,
They interpenetrate, play fast and loose
  With the world's crisp edges; pant awhile,
And then return refreshed.'

The crags from which illusion leaps
  Are real enough—and fast the chase,
But I've hurled rocks and failed to wipe
  That twitching grin from off its face.

The Dam Busters Norman Iles

From 'Sea and Fish Poems' Breakthru Publications

Men are the dam busters.
The dams are dames
In the lonely Harz mountains.
We dive down on them
One summer's night,
And bounce our bombs
Till we explode in spasms,
Deep in the water, out of sight,
Touching their curving curtain.

After the subsiding of the spray
A flume of loving energy
Shoots from their penetrated dyke;
Which would sweep away
All sleepers in the industrious Ruhr;
But for the potent finger
One man can use to stem the pressure.

Relief arrives for everyone
When these powerful reservoirs
Are dams of children.
Babies are bust blessers!
The foes become the best of friends;
And the war is over, till the next time.
We can make a film, or poem!

'*No Title*' John Beynon

holdhard and dontcry and kissnow
forget the light nailed under the door
eager to walk in with the stairs
your books are marking time
in rows around the room
and your mother with a stethoscope
is listening at the ceiling down below
ready to call TEA
while your father above has his
  ear to the floor
the parking meters say begone
and it is an offence to stay
my love
i will come like the morning paper
 stand sentry with the milk
 hop onto your window
peck to be let in
 siege like sunlight your cell
 so holdhard and dontcry and hushnow

Paras E. G. Firth

The fleeting ecstasy of crisis
Watching constellations of blue rings
Laze up in panic at the ventilators' maelstrom
Like gentle Jews to crematoria—
Mapping an indulgence and our martyrdom
With the benign euphoria of reefers—
Where eddying eyes and searching fingers
Meet and fix in quaking fellowship,
Sardonic and enduring as a death pact.
My dear, I guess we won't know till tomorrow
On what hapless island is this
Rumbustious old wreckers' haven
We have come to, niched on the north face—
Where, with saboteurs and Maquis
On the brink of Normandy, we wait
Besieged by gun-emplacements
In the famished dawn. Stealing
One another's blankets—chewed
By ferocious ants—and nagged
By stonechats and distressful kittiwakes,
Camped on the precarious
Ledges, seaward of some quarry's crater—
For grapnels of commandos
And the wraiths of landing boats

Object & Subject Jennett T. Stewart

O.K. I But I
am your am also
object, O your sub
and you ject plea
mine, mine ding for
our co-existence.
Do you not see
our piteous
fragmentati
on related
relentless
into unity
formless
void, un
placed
and un
dated?

Before June Benedict

Before disorder crept about
What a trail we blazed
Across two states.

You, always planting little
Trees
With no guarantee

They were evergreen-boughed.
And I love—nor could I
Promise beauty forever.

Mexican Christmas June Benedict

Indolent, languid yet serene
You stood, Saltillo
High on your windswept plateau
From the Rio Grande
We ascended your dusty slopes
And found a world unspoiled by man
Forgetting the pinched whiteness
Of a Michigan winter
Where the rumble and scramble
Of a big cities rush
Had crushed our souls
We expanded
Under the molten furnace of your orange sun
Which forged the scene, indelible
Unconfined, free as the circling falcon
And macaw overhead, we wandered
Hand in hand, mingling with brown
Barefoot children
Who chased striped iguana
Through tangled mesquite
Midnight in the moon-swept square
Spanish carols blended
With the eerie wail of wolves and coyotes
On some distant trail
Awaking the coiled sleeping fer-de-lance
Which slithered away
In search of its nightly prey
I plucked a scarlet poinsettia
To press in a book
So time to time I could steal a look
And we took our handful of days
Hurling them off eternity-ward
Today Saltillo
Some returned.

Thoughts

Brian Dormer Taylor

I had only four and a half hours sleep the night before
And the inert day with its narcotic hours
Invoked an unstable sunset beckoning the night
And ended the masquerade

I cried myself to sleep
Alone
Not too loud
In case anyone should hear
And asking why, mock or laugh

Look at that man who lost his left arm in a road accident
The nice boy who lives up the road
Blinded when a home-made rocket exploded
Smashing his face
And Mrs. Jones' sister with lung cancer
(And her only twenty-nine)
You're luckier than they

Luckier than they!
What dreadful lottery is this?

What are the hungry doing at this moment
Getting hungrier
And the prisoner in his cell
Lonely unloved
Sees a mocking image through the grille
The frightened killer after killing
Cannot rewrite history
Even if he
Wants to
History can only be changed before the event
If at all

What are the lonely doing at this moment
The lonely forgotten in aching rooms
Where the sun sometimes calls
To grin

Tell me God go on
You preachers and guardians of faith
Self-appointed teachers of truth
Luckier than they.

Sennen — Christina A. Savage

Do you remember the day in Sennen
When all the rocks held little pools
Of laughing water?
Where we tickled the fish
And teased the crabs
Who hid in hair-shadows
While Phoebus sent rainbows
Scudding through spray
Like fairy ships on an upturned sea?
Say you remember.

Barbarella — David Mycroft

Barbarella, high above the town
Ticks off the lights of London from her tower.
Ticks off Penultimate Harry, shambling Syd
Carcass Effendi, turgid Salvadore—
ticks off her lovers one by one
they click, they switch, they turn off
candelabra, tablelamps, luminous statuettes
and go to bed
because
Barbarella snaps her fingers thus
of her left hand.
And then she points with a finger of her right
A man emerges, blinking,
takes taxi, catches lift, knocks at door
summoned
and finally returns to bed
named.

Love — C. J. Randall

If twenty fags and twenty matches
Hold my icy bones together,
I'll keep your memory bright till morning
And slander not the birth of weather.

If one remaining railway sandwich
Keep my stomach's walls apart,
I'll hold you tight again in wishing
Bidding vision-food depart.

If the tap's metallic water
Stops this ashy throat from splitting,
I'll lay my soul for you to trample
And keep my manner more befitting.

I'll be a different lad come morning;
I'll be a proper little squire—
You buy me steak with pie for afters—
I'll throw my pride upon the fire.

The Real Thing — Tony Rand

On plastic walls
Plastic gods
Inscribe their plastic dogma.

On Christmas trees
Christmas stars
Glister with plastic horror.

The plastic toys
I played with
Have melted to oblivion.

The plastic girl
I played with
Has just had a miscarriage.

On Holiday — Grahame Smith

ladies and gentlemen,
at approximately 11 am
(on wednesday)
this little girl
leaned the devil out of a carriage
on this miniature railway
justso's she could see
the approaching train run over points
an' disappear behind an' after
into a tunnel.

at approximately 2 pm
this same little girl
on this rock
with some friend
threw stones (what the hell for)
into the sea
an' suddenly her hair blew sea sing
(so's she got flung accidently into beauty.)

Shades off, now, into hate . . . for each thesis has its antithesis—

Credo — Anthony J. Whittaker

Call me selfish; my tongue
stumbles over these chants of right and wrong.
I hold a diamond; my time
will give no other so truly mine.
Cut off my hand; how would you start
to prise my cold clenched fingers apart?
Few things are as this gem;
it is not in me to surrender them.

Equation — R. J. Tucker

Lynching naked necks
Is unjust to the hanging tree;
Judges pass by in tankard coaches
And remark at the poor man's fate
Reflecting that if that tree had not been
There. Then what?
The tree sweeps its arms in unseen protest
When the wind gives its freedom.
One rising morning—early in winter—
A headman's horse leaves the path,
Life bound to the tree.
Mutilated tree now burning away to warm others
—An equally unfair hearing.
A crowd's passion is like winter.

Rearguard Action

John Lovelace Street

Knaves and rapscallions,
  Morons and dunces,
Tatterdemalions,
  Man the defences.

The front line is broken,
  Picked men are running,
The citadel taken,
  Panic beginning.

Proud ones with banners
  Show the white feather.
Scenting their dinners
  Vulture packs gather.

You weak and unwilling,
  Without understanding,
A great mind is falling,
  Needs your defending.

Demons and ogres
  Stretch to infinity:
All Hell beleaguers
  Safety and sanity.

Knaves and rapscallions,
  Morons and dunces,
Tatterdemalions,
  Man the defences!

Mandelbaum David Mycroft

my name is mandelbaum
emeritus professor of statistics in the
  university of Yukon
passing this way
on an enquiry with an international bias
into the fecundity of homo londiniens
his habits
his habitats
his sexual proclivities
I have discovered that
1.27 londoners prefer blondes that minus 2.45
  of them prefer hermaphrodites
that the rates of sexual emission from ALL causes
within the Boroughs of Lambeth, Kensington and
  Buckingham Palace
are significant at the point nought one percent level
I have discovered in and out of my laboratory
that the male londoner thinks 2.9 times more
  often about food than intercourse
even when the figures have been partialled
  out to deal with sclerosis
silicosis and Crap's Disease.
my name is mandelbaum I am now returning to
  the united statistics of america
in a stratocruiser
at 4.57 miles per hour minnesota meantime.

Spring Etc.

Ronald Kerr

The fallows
all awash with mist,
white rain falls like sheets of pearl.

I loved that girl—
like the dark earth
she nourished me.

Now alone
I'm starved and howling.
The ploughboys have had her.

The white mare in the field turns
her dark hindquarters to the hot wind,
the furrows burn.

The pain of fertility
howls in her nerves and veins.
She runs wild.

Her mad teeth gnash.
Frustration's backlash,
barbed and bitter,

tramples over grass and flower.

Rose Window — Yvonne Abbatt

The sacrificing priest hieratic
towers at the altar, knife glinting
in the coloured filtered light
from the old rose window.
God! he's bungled it!
I can see it blinking.
Doesn't that creature mind being bungled?
It seems to acquiesce.

A Day — John Porter

There is a day of the dragon
when men's eyes flash
and their minds coil behind
like wreaths of smoke;
Days when the trees are statues
crystallised from the atmosphere
in fragile linking cracks.

A Truth? — Peter T. Smith

'You can't be moral
and be rich,'
I was told.
My pockets were found to be empty.
Can it be true?

Supremacy R. G. Gregory

Cat filthy with fleas and fatness
Far less white than white
From a night's free-lancing
In field and shed: scratching
Darkness off the windowed door,
The skin off my tender sleep.

Nature's harsh alarm, dragging
Conscience to consciousness;
Me from my bed's warm curl
To the scarred door. No thanks
From the prodigal intruder,
But an implacable pad through the house
For food. And finding nothing.

Caught between bed and the day
I follow, plugging the kettle in,
Fumbling haggardly for cups.
He runs a furry draught along my calves,
Miaowing bluntly. I let my foot
Flash in resentment; muffled
At once in fur, I bring it back,
The whole cat clinging to it
Warmly. A long slow purr
To pacify contempt. And—
'Get away you sod!' This time
He stays apart two inches
Licking his mouth, the raw
Ends of my sleep still rampant there.

My torn unwoken body
Prickles with rage; a thought
Unreasoning but horrified
Shivers against this creature
Barely my shin-bone high. Not cat
But creep of jungle shuffles there,
His cry man-eating, riling
The savage in me from its flimsy cage.
I get his food first, admitting fear,
Kowtowing to his purr. He knows his place
And makes of my supremacy a furtive thing.

20th Century Hymn Mick Hawes

If you're feeling dozy
And you need a prod
Don't take no little tablets
You need some GOD.

You say you're sorry
You'll start again
You sing a hymn
And you say AMEN.

You take a piece of bread
And a sip of wine
Say your prayers
It's COMMUNION TIME.

Chorus: There is a happy land etc. etc.

Night-Walk

David Goulding

I walked one night in town,
Passed 50 men if they were a day.
Walked past one who hated his wife.
Danced past another in love for the ninth time.
Stared at one who liked watching football,
Grinned at another without any money.

They all get hungry and eat.

Winked at one who just took a mistress.
Scowled at another because it's on Sunday.
One was boss-eyed—perhaps I'd been drinking.
Dragged past another who lived like a habit.

They all get thirsty and drink.

I jumped past one who was getting promoted.
Had a job getting past the one with eight children.
I smiled a bit at the one with no clothes on.
And I think I made the dog with the man itch.

They all get frightened and hate.

Neutrality

John C. Gilham

I have seen them:
Tangling, black, and utterly ridiculous,
From here just tiny pustules on the velvet cheek of sky;
And felt the wind,
And heard a distant thunder from the country of the blind.

And I have seen something else:
Stumbling, young, and utterly mindless,
A ragged woman with a baby at her breast,
Her breast,
Running, and running, as if the pain would never end.

And this is what I have seen:
Slavering, mad, and utterly powerless,
Clutching a case called 'Ministry of Defence',
A three-quarter man,
(He hadn't got any legs),
Who said, and said, 'Retaliate',
As if then he would walk again.

Smoke More Pot

D. M. Hopper

Smoke more pot.
Score more often.
Fix Fix FIX.
So the middlemen can prosper
And buy big cars
And have many women
Because the women will do anything
To smoke more pot
and fix more often.
So the traffickers can
get rich quick.
and live in style
In villas with nymphos
Who like the sweet life.
And don't smoke like you and me.
Pass the pot and the needle
Let's help all the people.
And smoke more pot.

A Lifetime of Scrawled Obscenities

David Weale

he sits
in the darkened cinema
coughing hoarsely
a cigarette hanging
from his lips like an indecency
while ash falls
carelessly
onto his coat
he is waiting
for the end
of the film

To the Ritual Celibate Bruton Connors

O murderous devotee
of defeated heats,
Cut off from liberty
In the franker streets,
Your stifled sons are jackals,
Shakily munching your intestines,
In the delicious night of love and crimes.

News Norman S. Jackson

This is the news. The house burned like a penny fizzer.
And one-year-old girl burned too.
Now let's talk about religion.
Now, lads; Isaiah—so called because
One Isaiah than the other—
(Come, come, Coggin. That's blasphemy—
or something) and the grapes-of-wrath type
Things are stored, and her little soul,
Her poor, little, little soul goes
marching? on—In a one-year-old scream
And a terror-burning heart-burst!
Yes. That was the news. Read by old
Who-cares. Now let's talk about religion.

The Jaws of the Poor Bruton Connors

A scarred man of the People,
A failure, broke and rubber souled,
I say to you, until you foretell
The lion in the garden, or the Venus in the swamp,
Until you presage hatred from company,
Or the melancholy of the sole man,
Until you have foreknowledge of cures in venoms
And deaths in pleasant beds,
Until you prophesy the wild lynx in the shrubbery,
Or the strangler at the pathway,
Until you name the glee or fate
In the wits of undone deeds,
Hang up your regret.

For one finds such crusts of fatalism
In the jaws of the Poor.

out of which love–hate dialectic grows a new synthesis. Our generation may not see it. Or they may. But it will arrive.

PROTEST

Protest! because 'he is a slave who dare not be/in the right with two or three . . .' and RACE—I race, thou racest, he *is a bloody racialist . . .*

Progress — John Bonnaud

Hear this! Hear this!
We drew angels,
they shouted, 'batman'.

We preached freedom
they said hang him.

We tried equality
They organised competition.

We worked to feed them
They cornered the market.

We said liberate
So they shot them.

We cried 'Our fathers'
They said buy candles.

We said laid to rest,
They said burn him.
Hear this! Hear this!

A Good Year Stan Rounds

Sixty-four was a very good year
for tyres, stereophonic pop groups,
the opposition party,
Liverpool,
Oh yes, and Geneva agreements
about somewhere.

Sixty-five was a very good year
for tyres, tunnels under walls,
the left wing,
Liverpool,
Oh yes, and a few spy planes
somewhere.

Sixty-six was a very good year
for tyres, sealing-wax records,
doctors emigrating abroad,
Liverpool,
Oh yes, and a few bombs
somewhere.

Sixty-seven was a very good year
for tyres, LSD, flowers and bunnies,
mild hippy weddings,
Liverpool,
Oh yes, and more bombs somewhere,
    somebody mentioned Vietnam.

Sixty-eight could be a good year
for bombs.

Parliament Peter Bradford

While another witty speech in support
of the latest Defence White Paper was
being given by the Minister to a full
house of God-fearing M.P.s bits of
bodies began to fall in their thousands
from the Parliament ceiling—toes fingers
feet hands noses teeth ears genitals
legs arms and this went on until Mr. Speaker
asked for the sermon to be discontinued and
by now the mound of body bits having attained
the mouths of the M.P.s stopped rising and
a gang of navvies were called in to remove the
avalanche of flesh to some high tip
overlooking a small Welsh village and when
this had been executed and the M.P.s were
promised compensation for the red stains
on their shirts and suits the Defence Minister
resumed his speech and Parliament on a
three line whip approved this year's defence
estimates by a large majority vote.

Extol the Unregarded Men

W. Stewart Rainbird

Extol the unregarded men;
Always the millions of unrewarded men,
the simple ones,
crafty with weapons, ploughs, and tools,
providers for, and protectors of nations,

Thor strokes in Panama, Simplon, Assouan;
multiples of finger-tips and hammer-taps;
Wrath of Jehovah; Hitler's, Joshua's, Haig's,
manœuvring feet of questing myrmidons:
always the millions of unrewarded men.

Ur was theirs, as Paris and Pittsburgh are,
angular templed Thebes, Rome road-radiant,
that marted Babylon, this bartering London:
Calloused palms on thighs the doers appraised
the manifest Truth in the made thing,
downed tools to oblivion:

god in the plumb column, the masonry firm,
the accurate ministration of engines;
god spurned in themselves.
Always, alas, the millions of unregarded men?

Witch-Hunt Harry Thomas

The sergeant said,
'He is suspect,
He receives letters,
From foreign friends.'

Hooked Olga Gibb

That's how they tricked you, slipped you the
Dark dope, and stole your brightness.
You looked for kicks and took the pricks,
Hurried beyond the threshold because you could not
Bear the proffered world of nightmare men,
Because we slept too long.
Who was it said . . . 'So many thousand years to wake
But will you wake for pity's sake?'

Sunday Papers — Cynthia Fuller

The gale had blown me awake.
Holding over nakedness a red dressing-gown
Into the street
Into the watery-wind I ran
Chasing papers blown in turmoil
From their respective doorsteps.
In separate sheets they flew
Caught like caged birds against railings
Masks over parked cars
White flags in the sky.
Sideways gliding somersault turning
They attacked me
In madness I grabbed them
In madness fought them
I alone was alive in the street
Snatching at these printed autumn leaves.
Crushing them in my arms
I staggered back into the house—
But when I came to read them,
They made no sense.

The Man in Bradford

Robert J. Pickles

He walks the city streets
awaiting a message
from the
Lord.
Open sandals and a brown robe
tied in the middle
by a knotted
cord.

He may be thirty-two;
What's that to you?

He stands and smiles,
blue eyes wide, at
passers-by.
Is that the light of truth
or madness
in his
eye?

And I hear the soft
but persistent cry:

crucify, crucify.

The Local Nicholas Caulfeild

Middle-aged and paunched
Bespectacled and merry
He perches upon his regular pint
Sized stool within the Red
Forever flowing Lion and commences to
Pronounce with slurred absurdly confident
Unknown fact upon some subject
About which he knows absolutely nothing;
And attended to by the entire
Entirely sozzled company with
Their ears and hear hears he raises
Once again his glass up to his
Slurping lips, and with it up goes the level
of the world's prejudice
And slops down upon the under spirit
Floor where ignorance is bliss
'tis folly to be wise,
While outside, the earnest nervous
Trembling truth teller
Is sitting at the door begging
For the unforthcoming money
For a drink
And wasting his young so
Sober wind upon
Their randy brandy breaths.

The Best Butter

Ian Duplessis

Like cobras, the slimy evasions
Glide, Laocoön-like, entwining
The tiny, tare-stifled plant.

The evasions, like the best margarine,
Are churned out fresh daily;
And their dairy-fresh smoothness,
Their consoling, justifying taste
Sink sublingually into the bloodstream
And there, silent, forgotten,
As effective as a heart-beat and as unconscious,
Distort nerve, feeling, vision.
The tares are old.

The astigmatic evasions poison the good gift,
The tiny tare-stifled plant,
Which lives.

Vocation Jimmy Barbour

Don't ask me, Mac,
Why he should call
Us out.
We're carpenters,
After all.
I know that normally ropes are used.
But what if we'd refused?
God knows what would've happened to us then.
We're only men—
Go here, go there,
Do this, do that.
So, no back-chat:
He'll give us thirty bob with any luck
(God! his coat is stuck:
They laid-on with those flails!)
You take his hands,
And I'll cross his feet—
We'll only need three nails.

Synthesis Timothy Read

Through my two eyes I see the world
In nature's nomad colours,
It is a world that welcomes men
Though men distort the colours
  so black becomes a 'nigger's' skin
  so white's a pure man's collar
  so greasy grey effects a 'yid'
  so yellow 'chinks' are squalor.

What if the sky dawned sick of green
Or the earth of blue-lit mornings—
We'd die all-in with one shortcut
No lengthy string for men's perusal
No envy to hate to kill to pity
No chance to play with anti-quitty;
We'd make a multi-coloured pulp
Only sighted sense could order
Till back we came to what we have
A world we shouldn't border.

Bird and Beast Wilfrid M. Appleby

Tim whistled all the while he worked,
  melodious as a singing bird,
oblivious that his music irked,
  or even that he could be heard.

His irritated foreman scowled:
  'You need a cage for that canary;
—how can I concentrate?' he growled.
  But Tim's good-temper did not vary.
Quietly, he said, with quick rebound:
  'You need a kennel for that hound!'

Sic Transit Cartwright Timms

They're playing bingo in the music hall
Where once, twice nightly, glittered all the stars,
Here tenors sang and red-nosed comics quipped,
Their ghosts move silently around the bars
Acrobat, juggler, comedienne and clown
George Formby, Little Tich and Harry Brown.

They're playing bingo in the music hall
Where once they sang of Devon by the Sea,
Where Barton rode his bike and Marie Lloyd
Followed the van each night so helplessly,
Gertie Gitana sang of Nellie Dean
And Vesta Tilley was the gallery's queen.

The music's gone, the violins are still,
The dressing rooms are empty and the flies
No longer hold the gaudy scenes. No more
The chorus dance and flaunt their shapely thighs.
Laughter and song have gone, beyond recall.
They're playing bingo in the music hall.

The Day the Machines Came Hadyn J. Adams

They said, 'Go get your cards.'
So I walked across to the personnel office.
Jenny was there.
'You too, Mr. Smith?' she said.
I forced a half-smile.
'Me too,' I quipped.
Bates, the P.O., stood and said nothing—
Just watched.
Suddenly he began, 'We're really terribly . . .'
But his last words were lost to me
As I walked out into the open air.
I was free—and that's what I hated most.
In 'The Plumed Serpent' D. H. Lawrence says,
'There's no such thing as liberty.
You just change one sort of domination for another.'
Well the domination of freedom is awful—
Just awful!
It scares me now that I'm free—
Forcibly free!

British Chivalry Eric A. Willats

Across gashed Italian heads
White handkerchiefs are bound;
On their knees they kneel,
Floppy arms upraised.
Weary, played-out tank crews,
Sludge-stained motor-men
With their black woollen caps,
Mechanics' oily overalls,
Oily brown skin; he, over there,—
Just stepping from his battered, captured tank.
Yes, just a puppet in War's sordid play.
Fought and was beaten and never ran away.
Marched, dragooned and driven
To a dirty, rotten fray.
See in some Sicilian town
Where the olives grow,
See the frenzied wife bow down
As her soul feels what she doesn't know.
Her brave garage mechanic,
Peace-loving citizen,
Giovanni Corregio, honest, lazy and mild;
Sunny-hearted, passionate;
They've caught him, 'Oh, my child!'
The dark-eyed infant sobbed and wailed.
And on the Gaumont-British screen
They showed him; how the bourgeois scream
With laughter: 'You taka da tank!
I sella da ice cream!'
   Oh, very funny,—but it stank!

On the T.V. Report of the Opening of the Ku Klux Klan in Britain

Robert Smith

'My argument is not with the nigger in the street,
but with the pigs who allow them in.'
So he spoke
(an old follower of Jordan)
of 'scum blacks,
Imperial Britain,
courage and blood,
Empire,
glory,
Empire,
glory,
and Socialist betrayal'.

My teutonic skin squirmed.

I have seen coloured men
kiss their children.
I have quarrelled with them
about bus fares,
dart scores,
colour.

I feel I know a little of their mystique—
something as yet free of the northern tautness,
the neurosis,
that has made us clamber
savagely and ant-like
over the world.

O.K. I'm a pig.

The Ballad of Malcolm X Robert Leach

Malcolm X was a violent man,
Hated by the respectable Ku Klux Klan:
His dad was sliced up on a railroad track
For the very good reason that he was black.

Malcolm X was a dope-stung dope:
He'd sell his soul for a drag of rope
'Cause he had to go somewhere away from life
And it was either that or a bright-edged knife.

    Malcolm X, Malcolm's black,
    Malcolm X, Malcolm's dead,
    Shot from the front through to the back,
    Shot through the belly and shot through the head.

Malcolm X was a layabout lout—
An idle, thieving, marijuana-tout—
So the white coppers said that he'd got to be done
And they put him in a prison where he couldn't see the sun.

Malcolm X was a clever git:
When he got out of jail he did a flit,
And he wasn't seen again till he was a preacher-man,
Shouting 'Respect!' for the dirty nigger-man.

    Malcolm X, Malcolm's black,
    Malcolm X, Malcolm's dead,
    Shot from the front through to the back,
    Shot through the belly and shot through the head.

Malcolm X was a bearded crab,
Scruffy and dirty—an American scab,
'Cause he never seemed frightened about what to say
Of the hypocritical platitudes of J.F.K.

Malcolm X was a dangerous guy,
The black man who above all must die,
'Cause he wouldn't give the white man his longed-for boost
And saw that the chickens were coming home to roost.

    Malcolm X, Malcolm's black,
    Malcolm X, Malcolm's dead,
    Shot from the front through to the back,
    Shot through the belly and shot through the head.

Malcolm X was a wicked man,
And must have been soft in his black brainpan
'Cause he wanted the nigger to be really free
In the Great Society of Lyndon B.

    Malcolm X, Malcolm's black,
    Malcolm X, Malcolm's dead,
    Shot from the front through to the back,
    Shot through the belly and shot through the head.

White kiddies won't be frightened when they're tucked up
        in bed
'Cause black ogre Malcolm is good and dead;
They'll go back to sleep when they wake up in the night
'Cause black ogre Malcolm can't give them a fright.

    Malcolm X said what he thought,
    Malcolm X lived what he taught,
    Malcolm X got what he bought—
    The black mouse in the white trap beautifully caught:
        White men snort
        But they'll be taught,
    'Cause Malcolm X didn't die for nought!

To Muhammad Ali: 22nd February, 1967

Arthur Charles

Torn from their Native Land your forbears groaned
  Beneath the white man's lash: their agony
  In suffering cries from unmarked marshy
Tracks: 'Blood for my blood whom blood enthroned:

Have they yet learned who've seen the Past in
  Future 'toned—
  That what is sown we all must reap? Ali!
  Your manliness—this only fools deny . . .
Astute—in fearless greatness—Johnson you discrowned.

Black Prince . . . Li'l Artha vindicated too;
  But in excess the hope of Wills forever
Crushed and harmed the Sacred Cause anew

  Save for all Fascist hordes—till higher
Hope of Man's humanity to Man you drew
  And they you from your Greatness would dissever.'

'Black Prince'—Peter Jackson, West Indian negro boxer. Never allowed to fight for heavyweight title, or would almost certainly have won it.
'Li'l Artha'—Jack Johnson, first coloured world champion, thus vindicated Jackson.
'Wills'—Harry Wills, the Black Panther, whom Jack Dempsey was not permitted to fight.
Muhammad Ali vindicated Jackson both as man and boxer; Johnson vindicated him more in achievement than character.

White is the Colour of my Dying Frame

Tony Rand

White was the colour
Of my bridal gown.
White was
The cake to be cut.
White was when people
Knew but his
Name,
And white is the colour
Of my dying
Frame.

Black was the colour
Of my true love's hair.
Black was
The day I met him.
Black was when they said,
Don't let him
In,
For black was the colour
Of my true love's
Skin.

Consideration Stan Rounds

Please take into consideration
the condition of the crazy paving,
no two lines meet,
and some cracks in places
are wider than in others,
you could get your foot caught in one
and fall hard upon that
which supports you.
Please consider the condition of the
crazy paving when falling,
no two lines meet,
by falling forward you could get
your fingers caught up in that
which supports you.
By falling backward there is a
greater danger of striking your head,
lying prostrate, almost unconscious,
and not surveying that
which supports you.
If you fall, make sure you fall
forward, and in falling,
please take into consideration the
condition of the crazy paving,
no two lines meet.

which breaks us, but could make us . . . and NATURE; but without corn . . .

Stupid — Graham Thomas

On the scrubbed front step
the milk bottles stand
sucked dry by hordes
of marauding birds.

And out in the garden
the prize blooms bend
unable to bear
the weight of cats;

But the police are seeking
a silent stranger
who likes his milk
and is jealous of flowers.

Muffin Vendor Roy Bennett

Every raw Sunday afternoon,
Sancho to the lamplighter's freewheeling
Don saluting glass skulls with a taper
Till they turkey-gobble and blurt moonstone
Embers, he humps his tray akimbo, honing
His toasts and dry clapper away to the colour

Of cold, banging ice-holes in the sharp sky.
Prompt still for all change, through a cleft palate
He wheezes, and dabs his peg leg
On the same yet not the same roadway,
Tarred graft of another planet
Patched over the blaze that took his dog.

This brass-tongued tintinnabulum
Rings back that bright eye with six million Jews
Out of the oven, and how many hundredweight
Of corpuscles that chilling dawns consume
Out of the ashes of that sulphurous
Dusk. Suns bulge the cracks of his black coat.

Warehouseman

Lette Heselton

Presumptuously, I pitied him
who like a half-blind dusty mole
emerged at six o'clock to sniff the day
and disappeared down a different hole.

His billowing smoke for sky; black
skittle chimneys in the haze,
the opaque canal too tired to flow
its factory-canyoned waterways.

Staccato chirp of urchin sparrows,
loud claustrophobic press
of lorries, breath of hot alleyways
scorching the concrete nakedness.

He said: 'This is my home, I like
this street and its familiar faces.
Green fields are fine for countrymen and cows
who enjoy silence and open spaces.'

Don Mario Borelli's Family

Margaret Perkins

The Scugnizzi, unwanted flotsam
polluting Naples' gutters.
Filthy, tattered, human debris;
stunted, rickety men of six
and ageless youths.
Self-exiled from teeming hovels
they scrounge in bins
with alley cats;
forage cigarette butts;
lounge insolently in corners,
half tensed for flight.
Fitful, frosty nights,
huddled on pavements,
have bonded them hirelings
of vice and crime.
Two new Scugnizzi tomorrow
quickly compensate
for the solitary
suicide today.

Piccadilly Tube Station

William Limmer

Under Eros
The homeless millions hide
In anonymity.
The heart's great problems slide
Into a mirrored happiness
As brittle and as cold
As love's hour-glass:
All things must pass.
Mirror, mirror on the wall,
Where is my lover nine feet tall,
With honeyed tones
And honeyed eyes?

Under Eros
The rootless millions ride
In equanimity.
And fogs disintegrate,
Divide, reconstitute
As dreams
Under a thousand sodium suns
In rock-cold streets above.
Tell me, tell me,
What is love?

Plot Forgotten—and Forgiven

James George Johnson

Cato Street you haven't changed
The days long gone since your
Infamous plot stopped short its
Tracks in bloody battle;
A Judas spoke and to Newgate
Did your scheming tenants go
The dead to hell or heaven for
The country's living foes.
Your heart remains cocooned
In time your body long since
Changed its shell, your
Story long since lost its
Desperate edge for now in
Word and sight of you your
Tenant holds the key
To your unchanging door.

Unchanged by change
Protected not by lucky fame
A gifted son, a house that held
In deathless memory a treasured
Host that dares defy
The all-embracing eye of time,
And builder's wanton hammer.
What credits you your lack
Of blows in this an age of
Pain for brick, to what or
Whom do you own your island
Luxury a builder's debt? a sudden
War? plans lost in dust or
Servants' straying thoughts.

Public Service: 1966

Molly Partis

They used to emerge in the olden days,
From the mines, from the bowels of the earth,
To taste the purer air of verdant fields,
And blink away the dust from down below.
She, too, was escaping, short and plump in
Her protective nylon overalls, arms
Folded, having left her territory
Heavily disguised with disinfectant.
She too came up for air, not pure, not dust free,
For the entrance to her burrow was in
The middle of a main road, polluted
With exhaust fumes and the stench of petrol.

Bus Stop

Arthur D. Clegg

The lorries hum
Through Islington
And in the din
A man may sing
Something absurd
And not be heard
In Islington.

Dead End and Not Coming Back

Timothy Read

The moon is large
                    and round
                                and lost
To the banalities of cream cheese;
Under here is where lovers stop,
Whose bearded serenadings live in bliss
Immune to death's cold, unquestionable hug.
  High over sings the storm-cock in its pastoral setting,
  Sings its throat to parchment
        and to envy
  Of flowers guzzling in a bedroom vase
Apart from the faded scent of extravagant kisses.

The moon is large,
                    and dry and warm
Is its overcoat hung over biers matted
With chatwood bones, feathers plucked, biceps
Freed of strength that held the willing party down.
                                                    Down
And gasping for an answering call, as wrenched
From the envious piper's warning.

Common Names — Gillian Bence-Jones

If names of woods and fields and land could conjure you,
Could carry you to them, could sing or say
The High Tree, Hobbin's, Burneville Hall;
Could give a part of what they give to me,
You'd be enraptured too; you'd murmur them,
The Hilly Meadow, Ladywood, Lark Hill.
But it's impossible, you don't recall
The Primrose, or how the blackbird sang
In Cuneford's, in Buss's Carr, in the Decoy.
And they who walked before in these green fields
Beneath the flowering thorn, their names remain
In Widgett's Walk, and Weathers', and Palmer's field.
Sir William Burneville comes into Domesday book;
I can remember Buss. The rest walked in between
The Straight Road, Plumptywent, Colomer Point.
I hope they are allowed to come back now and then.
I know I would come back from Heaven if I could
To Goldsmiths, to Thornywood, to home.

Road Signs Dilys Henrik Jones

For miles now the road ran through
The forest edge,
And always we saw signs,
Clear in any language—
The atavistic image from the nursery tales,
The long, lean shape.

Not that we met anyone who'd seen,
Himself, a wolf;
One man's father, long ago, had done so,
And there was always a boy,
But he had lived in the next village—
Or so they said.

Nevertheless they kept the signs new painted,
After all one never knew
In some dark, frozen winter they might come,
Once more, the wolves.

Primitive Patricia Martland

I am alone with fear
  in a world that is afraid
I hold my own too dear
and danger is prowling near
  my tribal bird-winged glade
  I wait the horrible raid.

Poisoned Sea Brian S. Pratt

Even the mighty sea is drowned in society's sludge.
Once crested waves fall back before the oncoming mire.
And the birds of the sky swoop down and die,
In a thick nightmare ocean of destruction.

The shimmering beaches once so free,
Now lie stained by machine blood.
The sky dark man-made clouds fill.
The earth covered by hard carpets of tar.

Hear the wind's plea, the rain's tears
Cry for life as the executioner comes near.
The ghost of freedom screams warning
To Man, the next for the death sentence.

Slug F. W. Flemen

after the rain
the grass
is green glass,
washed of shadow.
a sleek black fat slug
drags
itself along
stretching and shrinking,
intense, sinuous, menacing,
solitary.
its ugliness
so glistens,
its supple undulations
are so graceful,
its skin
so special polished
as to amaze my casual glance;
it slowly
shyly
waves
its short soft horns,
exploring the suave evasive air.

i fell
at once into its trance,
its spell.
i wished
there were some means,
some fashion
by which i could show
my passion.
my marvellous soul
aches
that such innocent sensuous creatures
should bear
such brutal, beautiful names.

Weeding

Joan Jordan

Weeding the worlds
At ant level
Grass a forest
Every weed
Jungle tree and savage bloom
The path a desert
One could die
Finding the other side.

The Rat of Tok-Chong

Bruton Connors

At Tok-Chong, a rat,
Cropping dust on the highway,
Saw the assassin
And the stone smashed him sideways.
As the lorry started,
He hid in the space
Of the hub and the tyre.
He spun for five seconds
Inside the wheel
And as he dropped out,
The second rock broke him.
He entered and spun
Four times and dropped out,
Then as the stoning continued,
Small, dusty, and insane
He died.

Au Bord de l'Eau Maurice Wilkins

(From the French of Sully-Prudhomme)

Sit we together beside a stream which flows,
  Watch it flow by;
Together, if a cloudlet flying goes,
  We'll watch it fly;
Watch, where a cottage roof smokes far away,
  The smoke curl up;
Where fragrant flowers embalm the noontide day,
  Their fragrance sup;
Where some rich fruit is tasted by the bees,
  Taste of its riping;
Listen, where a bird among the listening trees,
  Pipes, to its piping;
Hear, at the willow's foot, where water chides,
  The waters chiding;
Feel not at all, while the rich dream abides,
  Time the abiding;
No passion from the heart's deep wells we'll bear,
  But for each other;
The troubled world of men, its strife and care,
  In our souls smother;
We'll know, oh, we alone, where all things tire,
  Tireless and gay;
Where all things earthly pass, our hearts' desire
  Pass not away!

The Witch Peter Baker

Blowing
chill, the silver-wind morning
airs its dawn
above frosted thatch, crisp
swallows fly as confidently
hours uncover day.
She
grasps the tremble of this morning
and its life, moving
slowly
old and oddly sentient
along moss-softened path.
Stirring
leaves quietly, turning
swallows dive for safe eaves
as her eyes
prickle them aware,
whisper 'wicce'.

Sutherland Alfred McClintock

Is there another land
Like Sutherland
Of glistening lochs and lochans?
Is there another mountain
Like Suilven?
Oh, from this height
Unparalleled sight:
To look over
To Stac Polly
Culbeg and Culmore
And down
To the shimmering waters:
—These jewels are become
My soul's fetters—
Is there another land
Like Sutherland?
Another mountain
Like Suilven?
Here is my treasure
I will prize for ever.

Requiem for Ann — Pete King

Now,
  the Windmill
Stands,
  stubbed on the moor
Alone,
  with the owl-wind
  hooting at the door
Brushing,
  the silk fly nets
  spidered on the sill
Searching,
  with quick hands
  for the lost sails
  that shivered and died
Fell,
  with Ann
  in the hurt gales;
  and only an owl cried.

Rains Come — Ronald Kerr

Rains come.
Gone the rainbow
but the chemical substitute
ain't no better
no worse
just gaudier
tasteless
trivial.

The dawn
pulled
across the horizon
by two jets.
The night
pulled down
by twin engines
eight miles high.

Winter — Simon Stelfox

Winter walks in white and grey
And mourns in black.

Slow tears of melted ice
Make a meagre watercourse
Through a monotony of sombre snowfields.

A stunted pine
Holds forth a withered branch of ragged tufts
That some stony wind might sing a mournful
tune therein,
If so it will.

All else is still,
And sleeps with dreams
As colourless as deaths.

and because—above all—that is what we believe in—TOMORROW.

Mohandas Gandhi and the Onion Pickers

David Gill

Mohandas Gandhi, third-class traveller on Imperial trains
First picked the locks of shackled peasants with a safety pin.
Mohandas Gandh, bare-legged as the labourers
Walked nimbly through the dust of India's grievances.
Mohandas Gandhi, the mahatma, raised the eyes
Of the indigo-pickers of Champeran to the forgotten hills
Of self-esteem; he drove the gentle elephant
Of justice through the court-rooms, breaking furniture,
Apologising in advance not afterwards.
Mohandas Gandhi fed the thirsty continent
From the melted snows of his Himalayan heights of conscience.

Now why did all the peasants in Kheda district cheer
When Mohanlal Pandya, disciple of Mohandas Gandhi
And eight good friends plucked onions in the punishing sun?
They cheered because the government had seized the crop
To pay for revenue poor peasants would not pay;
They cheered at dusk when all the illicit roots were pulled,
And when the laughing onion-thieves were led away
The peasants cheered again, and in the solemn court
They cheered the culprits and the magistrate next day.
When Mohandas Gandhi saw his followers again,
He said: You have drawn the stubborn roots of the people's fear,
Who knows what onions we may one day have to pick?
When men go cheerfully to gaol, repression loses heart.

Three Japanese Fishermen Terence Strachan

'The weeping heavens over Christmas Island
Poured deadly hail upon our backs
And broke our loins (the fishing-nets
Hung loosely over the burnished decks).

The volcano god spoke from the clouds
Above the coral islands in the South
And mushrooms sprouted in the skies
Above our heads, in whirling O's!

The breeding-grounds among the atolls
Will breed a cancer in our blood
And in our seed; in future generations
A lonely traveller on this planet

(Wandering through empty space
As dead as Mars, in purple canals)
Will find a broken epitaph:
Here lies the last survivor—

Unless the peoples teach the arts
Of peace to warlike men.'

1946 Elizabeth Stuttard

'But when the great thaw comes
How red shall be the melting snow, how loud the drums'
DAVID GASCOYNE: SNOW IN EUROPE

No. In six years of war blood could flow red no longer
And drums belong to glory. This was no warriors' funeral;
In the end, no great sense of death;
Too many dead. They opened the cold ovens,
Decently buried what remained in cemeteries or in living
  graves—
The new camps, dumps of tin, barbed wire and sacking
That cross the no-man's-land of Europe.
Grey trucks, two bricks and a biscuit tin, thin soup,
The huddled line of spectres who should have died.
Behind them in the dust, a million more look on
Who disintegrated somewhere above Japan
In a moment of surprise.

Displaced. The war office has a word for it.
A network of fine red lines in a map room,
Zones, sectors, frontiers to mould a field of mud,
The new front line of the cold war.
The victors cheered, lit bonfires, danced in the streets
One night. The embers did not last them to tomorrow.

Hiroshima John Beynon

hiroshima
you are a beautiful girl making love
out of her skin

hiroshima
you are the desert of the black rain
and on your river live the dead

hiroshima
you are a hiding in folded arms
when our eyes shake hands with the sun

hiroshima
you are the contour of a man
burnt into the steps of a bank

hiroshima
you are the rising cloud
we wear in our head
and cannot leave on the chair
when we climb into bed

hiroshima.

Teach-in David Gill

In Oxford where the blackbirds sing
Among the pale dons' apple-trees
We watch the tiny Vietnamese
Perish on our telescreens.
Some people came to give us reasons
Why the programme
Shouldn't stop.

Poppy Day Contradictions

Jacqueline Pointer

Unreal these poppies
That we wear like badges.

(Every year I buy these flowers,
Knowing that we have to care.)

Better they should bloom in fields,
Bright, transient, fragile,
As real poppies are.

Better again a wand should wave,
And we should see churned fields
Of torn-limbed soldiers,
Remember sundered vows of: 'War no more!'

(Vows that were made in ignorance of powers,
Adolf, Adam-old despairs.)

Blobs of blood are poppies.
Unreal these poppies that we wear.

Peace has an Angry Throat Bella Cameron

Peace has an angry throat,
Has stopped singing.
The instruments gutless. The ampoule empty
Amnesty runs amok and performers suffer idiosyncrasies
Of promoters employing guilty managers,
Using key words in constitutional minutae.
Captivating peace wears price on head
When hunters know the score, the rest on balance.
Creditors clamour. Vultures hover.
Destruction promises that we come and go from amoebal.
The bomb grows spiritual anaemia. Gathers momentum
When ambitious peace suffers inhibitions
Backgrounds hoopla. Playgrounds smoulder.
Peace your freight is light. Your rolling stock
On probation.
Dumb guards are hoarse with answer. The unhappy face
Of peace holds honorary rank in monosyllables.
Changeling programmes hold pockets of indifferent renewal.
White elephants find few stalls.
Peace stallions stampede seeking title while donkeys
Put to plough.
Time watches wear leering faces.

Out of this Cave — M. Munro Gibson

Peace in the dark cave,
Where Man's ingenuity
Has lighted a fire,
And men from four caves stand and wonder,
United round this marvel.

A small peace this,
And it did not last,
For soon there were cities to burn.

Peace in the vast sky,
Where Man's ingenuity
Has launched a rocket,
And all Earth's nations unite to scan
This conquest of another planet.

Peace beyond the moon,
Where all Earth's rivalry gathers,
And the rockets carry no bombs.

Cain — Jacqueline Pointer

The average human creature wears
Rose-tinted thoughts to blur his cares,
But Cain through vice or virtue sees
Blood-rosy tints in common trees.

War on War

Mick Bunting

Fight the war against war!
Fire shells of charity at all nations;
Let each be struck a mortal blow
With the steel blades of reason.
Torture men with thoughts of progress.
Lock them in the dungeons of their
own black-heartedness;
Lash them daily with rods of liberty.
Invade all lands with bands
Of people-loving people, for these,
Not lovers of power and money,
Are peace-loving people.
Unleash the mighty force of peace,
Whose presence in men's hearts
Casts the weapons from their hands,
And the war from their souls.

'The Bronze Horseman'—Leningrad (A Ballet Featuring Peter the Great).

Louise J. Rosenberg

I sat up in his royal box
And saw upon his stage
A Czar of all the Russias
Framed in his golden age.

For golden are great Peter's domes
Along the Neva's banks:
Throughout this gracious city
They lie in broken ranks.

Broken by the echoing
Of tramping, suffering feet:
Of war and revolution,
In victory and retreat.

Yet the blood-red path of suffering's
Obscured by a silver glow;
For the cosmonaut is soaring
Through the gold of long ago.

In Towns Men Come Together

Patricia Martland

In towns men come together
with others of like kind
if that be their wish.
Scientist with scientist,
poet with poet,
painter with painter,
etcetera etcetera.
And with unlike kind
if that be their wish.
Like or contrary
can spark ideas off
till minds ignite
and hearts can see their way
clear through walls,
under streets, above the smoke
to build better.

Sociological Study 1: After Russell

Alec Cornwall

God came down to Trafalgar Square,
Preached peace to the multitude gathered there;
While quoting his sermon on the mountain
Four cops kicked him into the fountain,
Saying, as they ducked his head:
'This guy's a medieval beatnik red!'

History, Geography and Anarchy — Ian Lennon

A map of the world is a series of lines, invented by politicians
And armies.
Which new politicians (and armies) change from time to time.
Without consulting people.
If you were born on one side of a line, and I the other,
You would be one nationality, I another.
You may be taught to hate me,
And I taught to hate you,
By the politicians.
You may have to defend your line;
Against me!
Without regard for people in between,
When we are older.

A place or area enclosed by a line is called a country,
By the politicians.
Not the people?
I live in a country, and so do you.
'Your' country wants 'Mine',
Wants to move the lines.
Or so I have been told
By the politicians.

One day the people will rub out the lines . . .
And the politicians.

Newsflash Helen MacGowan

There are too many newsflashes
Telling, over the air, of multiple disasters.
An emotionless voice uses set words
For momentous, and frightening, statements.
Tragedy is arresting, is compelling;
While happiness eludes the headlines,
And contentment, being unremarkable,
Is never figured in statistics.
But there came a day when,
Taken by surprise,
I heard the measured, flattened voice
Reading news which was wholly good.

'For the first time in seven years,
Rain has fallen on the Kalahari desert;
And a pilot, flying over it,
Observed that the desert was green.'
You deserts of Negev and Sahara,
Of Gobi and Antarctica,
Take hope from Kalahari!
Nursed in dry dust, the seeds lie sleeping,
Waiting for terrestrial miracles.
Let men become midwives to deserts,
And new peoples shall feed on old desolations.

The March of the Gods M. L. Jordan

Saturn, that poor senile king,
once lost his throne to lusty Jove,
a son of vigorous ambition.
He too bore the print of mortal mould
and suffered aging with the passing time.
So when the lustrous ebony of his beard
gave way to flowing snow,
the novelty worn off
by constant friction in the minds of men,
another youthful son of J.V.H.
rose up to carpet bloody battlefields
with lilies of Elysian fields of peace.
The lilies overblown, sedition sown,
men martyred him and nailed him to the tree
that showed his self-denial of the prime of life.
He died a mortal death, still young,
and for his sacrifice was honoured
with much longer youth, denied the rest,
whom immortality made old.
But now is he too aged;
his face has lost the haloed hue,
his beard is covered by the snows of time
and man must once again create
a god in his own likeness.

An Atheist's Prayer Sean Healy

I want to live,
to see the flower's opening lips
drink in the Summer's rain,
and not,
the frightened eyes of orphans
crazed with pain.
To see,
the golden moon rise up above
the distant hill,
A lover's moon,
and not a bomber's, out to kill.
To hope,
that man shall follow man
as has happened since the race began
and that the line
continue endless till the end of time.
No god or gods I ask for help,
Let men appeal to men,
'Give us this day our daily bread'
Not bombs . . . Amen . . . Amen.

Diggers' Song: 1649 — Arthur D. Clegg

How many lives I hold in my hand
With this earth, with this root, with this flower
I, as I breathe, as I move, as I tread
On other men dead
As I read, as I speak, as I sing
How many men

Jungle and swamp this land
Where the gnarled oak stood
Where the grey wolf drank
Where the great bear killed
This bare hill
Where the houses rise.
This flower was weed
Till someone chose
And did

I in my hands ten thousand lives
I in my speech their deaths
Humanity they made
Community displayed
Prosperity they prayed
They sit on my tongue
They wield my spade

Fire Power Connie Ford

When among the first men
Some bold spirit
Claimed you for his own,
Fed you, and tamed you
He looked back into his cave
And saw himself
Black, and ten feet high
Against the soft warm-lighted depth of rock.

This was that insatiable monster
That swallowed Troy,
That devastated London,
This was the death that smote Hiroshima.

I saw a gardener's face, kippered and kindly,
Intent above his bonfire.
There lies hope.
If only gardeners outnumber generals
And train you to their ways,
Pruned, bright, and fragrant.

'Everybody wants to go to heaven, but nobody wants to die' . . . and, JUST poems . . . which means: to poems that mean so much, we're —unjust.

From a Railway Carriage Harry Tomlinson

Slower than fat slugs, cursed by witches,
Slums and dumps, slagheaps and ditches,
And crawling along like troops in the trenches
All through the back streets it lurches and wrenches.
All of these sights of the dirt and the pain
Are happily hidden by black driving rain.
And here again, the glance of tired eye
Sees unpainted stations; I heave a sigh.

Here is a child who was wandering dreaming
All by himself, scrambled and screaming.
Here is a tramp, now trapped by the law,
And there was the green for hanging the poor.
Here is a car run away in the road
Heading for death with the man and load.
And here is a prison and there is a beck,
Each is a glimpse of a town that's a wreck.

Stage One M. W. Ramsden

A complexity
so acute
defies
articulation
couched in
vague ideas
they say
today
pragmatic
and feeling
as I do
it's hard to act
feeling as I do
I seem to feel
that what I do
is difficult
because
motives
principles
(all my own work)
come first
a dogmatic
insistence
on what I feel
I start with
this always
work outward
and ask
is eating lobster
with sauce
as bad
as drugs?

Man of Steel — Allan Peel

Barney Richards!
Now there's a lad for you!
You'd think he looked pretty dim, till
A jerky grin lights up his face like
The winking light on an advert sign.
It's a funny thing, he always has a terrible thirst;
He can down nine pints in an hour and a half,
And can still argue like a learned judge, and
Seems to talk more sense than some of them!
And another thing—he's always pushing
And tugging—like an overgrown lamb at the
Udder of an unwilling ewe at a slot machine
Installed in the 'King William' where he's
One of the regulars, trying to win top prize—
A gallon can of beer.

That's what comes of being weaned too early, I reckon!

Not that there's anything soft about Barney.
He's a turner, a man of steel, who shapes that
Metal to his will, with strong broad hands.
I sometimes think that some of the shavings
That fall from his lathe have entered his soul,
He's so calm and stolid.
A keen blue eye for the girls has Barney,
He likes to sample their wares,
Beguiling eyes, soft lips, firm breasts.
He leaves them in no doubt about what
They might have thought, at first, was a cosh!
Ay, a rare lad is Barney!

Absolute Despair James Dempsey

The happy lorry trundle will not come tomorrow,
The neon-trucker's out of gas & I'm clean out of
    sorrow,
I could bum a ride off a 10-ton truck but my
    way is much too narrow
For anything larger than a pair of feet & a
    selfish helpless sparrow.

Interlude No. 5—Sun and Moon
George T. R. Cairncross

Daedalus and Icarus flew
out in the midday sun,
and are only remembered
in Legends of Ancient Greece
passed on from generation to
generation.
A hydra-headed hyena howls
at the blood red African
moon. The night is filled
with the roars of preying
savage beasts roaming
over the blood-drenched soil
like a ledger sheet spilling
over with overdraft red.
Liabilities outweigh assets
in the jungle of survival
and in the end the strongest
are also lost as their assets
turn sour.

In the Still Summer Heat — A. C. Landor

In the still summer-heat the old woman died.
  The flowers were out in the noon-day blaze,
The girls swung their skirts, and cruelly played
  the children, whilst the man walked with a stony face
alone and forlorn, no longer a part
  of this earth and its frolics with his shattered belief.
He sleep-walks alive with a broken heart
  and carries like a corpse the burden of his grief,
His aged eyes well with still-born tears
  less for the dead than the loneliness he fears.

Three Haiku

Anthony E. Harckham

The still of dusking day;
The noise of engines
Betokens moving men.

*

The first pale fronds of lunar light
Silvering the sylvan scene;
Life freezes still.

*

A long black cloud across the night sky;
Lights shine below,
A myriad.

Rodin's Bronze 'L'homme au Nez Cassé'

N. G. Maroudas

You! Head with a soul trapped in!
Lacking body, lacking equilibrium,
In youth rolled headlong downhill with your companions,
Hit by people and things, frightened by loneliness,
Rolled down an endless incline with your companions,
In an avalanche of broken stones.
Came to precarious rest, helpless on the ground,
While a slow, corroding wind, the poisonous
Time corrupted you.

Safe now in the museum, in this stiff, crooked attitude,
Regard the casual world, the casual slaughter;
Look through your battered mask of bronze
From soft, blank eyes, that have no pity,
Have no hate: 'I am a man
More sinned against than sinning.'

th mouth of my sunday suit

Robert Fearnley

o th scrounger that i am
denied
        my silver
moon in moods of th sunniest
  shame
i ever bathed my yawnin
eyes in
        pullin smiles
outa th pockets frayed round
th mouth of my sunday suit
eatin
        everythin they
give me and pourin coffee over my
burnin tongue to satisfy it
before
        i prostitute
my poems for their payment

thank god i left my mind hangin
in th cupboard with th
  comfortable
clothes of
        my sailboat life.

After School

J. D. Goodger

a playing field of feet everywhere
slurred in the new snow and
just left about for the sun to weak
on
The foot makers are all gone now
gulped up by buses
  It was some manypede from the Ice Age
  grinning at January
  that shed all these feet
  (while no one was looking)
Soon a little man with a pointed stick and a pulled-out
  shadow
will come out
and prod at them etc
and spear them all up
and stuff them in a sack

Analogue

John Porter

Has ever a clay model
reached pseudopodial about itself
to mould its eyes to face forwards
its ears to be deaf.
He will make the shell
make it solid,
and poke out the filling
as an unnecessary suicide circuit.

Elegy for Taffy Pete King

I have heard
The tap, tap, tap,
Of the woodpecker in the wood.

It tapped thrice to tell Taffy
The time had come
And his Meteor blew up
Over the Sussex Downs
And a shower of silver fell all around.

Only a song,
And the mad thrush
Who lifted his head in the blackberry bush
Sings on:
Only a song,
Only a song.
And the woodpecker pecks holes
In his Sussex boles
Oblivious of death lying on the ground.

Silence — Margaret Kenmore

This silence speaks to me as with
a voice
I wish it were a language that I
knew,
There is urgency within the very
sound
That seems to warn and plead, yet
menace too.

I grow uncertain as I listen now,
So strange it is that silence can
be heard,
And my uneasiness is tinged with
fear;
Yet who can say if I have heard a
word!
If all is still and yet I hear these
sounds,
And now my dread is that I may be
right,
What may I not have lost to miss
the sense
Of these strange words that come to
me tonight.

Home Norman Humphreys

A room where shadows fall short
Space is improbably filled,
Cases piled high on the wardrobe
Filled with the contents of a cupboard
That space does not allow.
Walls covered with memories.
Light from a single lamp
Bright at source, darkness
Clings in the depths of hidden corners.
An awkward shape
For any room to be
Alive only when the human
Contents breathe the desperate
Pulse of need through
Its flimsy framework.

Stones John Porter

Stones and other things
live as statues to words
praising the sound of sticks
  uncarved
pebbles uncut.
In the beginning
was it the word
or the beach ?

Observation 3 B. Owen Fairbairn

The neurosis-clad little man
  plunders himself for sins
that he dare not carry out.
  The innocent, yet guilty girl
looks deep to find solace
  for the things she will do.
The man-about-town
  with his winning ways
knows he has it made.

The gossip-spitting old maid
  knew better days but
now knows jealousy for what it's worth.
  The curate with his benevolent smile
looks sideways at the collection box
  drawn in with willing hands.
The mechanism of life turns
  like the rusted cog wheels
of a three-wheeled bus.

The silent sitting thinker
  hangs on the edge of dreams
but does nobody any good.
  Gospel cries like broken promises
Carried on the wind that cares not
  nor blows anyone good.

I stand alone, no comparison
  to any but a similar soul—
Waiting to be overtaken.

Frequency 7 Michael R. Hunt

FRE——7 rings you up;
beats you
  hands
    down
and out for the count. 7
hangs you up
  on yourself
        frequently.
and then again
frequency 7's
    the big, slow beat
 that'll crack your wa–ll
      make you
             fall
violently in bed
   through your head.
        it's a gass
so you'd better die
    laughing
split your
sides
  on 7
  brides   for
   their brothers in law
  are gonna score.
frequency 7 beats on
        your door
frequency 7 burns the
             floor
frequency 7 is psychic &
             slick
—gets you sick
  and a whole lot more
  gives a kick
      licks you quick.

Time Stands Still — Keith Armstrong

time stands still
   on this bleak hill,
but ripples elsewhere,
   time moves by this bleak hill
but moves slowly
   everywhere.

time stands still
   not by this hill,
who's to care?
   but moves quickly
nowhere.

time stands still
   on this low hill,
who bears?
   the past flying swiftly
somewhere.

time stands still
   on this dry hill,
who dares?
   to cry sharply,
anywhere.

Eleven Lines in Prayer — Derek May

Tomorrow
you will escape into and become
a drinker of beer, smoker of fags
happy that your wife is thirty years from death
and that there is money for the funeral.
Unmoved by the distant suffering,
although you will pity them no doubt
whilst you're waiting in some supermarket queue.
As one who hates and loves in unequal parts
I sit in judgement on all of this
and wish each day to be yesterday.

No Grey Days Judy Upton-Kemp

Hate or love.
I walk in deep valleys or stand on the top
of a high mountain.
There are no flat lands of like.

Enemy or lover.
I run from a thunderstorm, or bask in the
hot sun. My outlook is never an overcast
average.

Desperate or ecstatic,
I stumble through dark woods, or tread deep
in yellow cornfields. I never see the
heatherclad moor of apathy.

Black or white.
I am blind; or all is clear to me.
I never see greywise through everyday eyes.

Conscience R. L. Parsley

Reds swim
Blues float
Yellows strike
In that dress
You look like a shark.
Where are your teeth?

Time

Terry Kingham

Time
Creeps into corners,
Settling there.
Slithers on, with
snake cunning, to where
Only the tense, possessive fears
of Lovers notice it.
Time, too, possesses,
takes, like Lovers, only
with a greater subtlety.
Time has placed a stranger
here, in my head,
Taking special care
To name him after me.

A Surrealist Painting by Bill Crook

Peter Jury

Superimposedly pitchered
The black head lies;
The supplanted optic by staring design.
The clean green is free
But Hades has its guest,
The black slime remains
Where Pluto stood.
No use now to break down the frames
The oesophagus all unreceptive.

Perspective John Bonnaud

There'll come a time
when that jet blasting past
will be outdated as
the clip-clop horse

For all our pride in technical progress
a future man will raise an eye
as he lets his mind regress
to our technical finesse

He'll laugh and say,
'They were a funny lot.
Surely they could have seen
that I . . . .'

To My Dog Everard Flintoff

To my dog, nose down, the present is
Never cobalt. No distance is.
Objects are sniffing: mind the flash
of sagas of redolence, yesterday's
fights, the diagonal scurryings of
fidgety minute life, events
in monochrome dated by their vividness.
To my dog, an epithet's a sort of ghost,
to hunt is to end whose haunting.

Clock Robert J. Pickles

That clocks watches me;
it stands serene
beneath a glass dome
on three green pillars
like a miniature
Wellsian monster.

When will it strike?

A Thinker Robert Smith

When a bus window flashed sun
in its speed
I thought of sea—
surging,
bursting
curls of sea.

When a sparrow
trembled with all its song
on a T.V. aerial
I thought of trees
leapt with birds,
shone with leaves.

When I felt the narrow pavement
I thought of grass
shining like sun on water.

I'm a powerful thinker
on five or so pints.
They make me hungry
in the flesh—
ready to taste.

I'm as mundane as my environment
and anything
might produce a great thought!

Cosmonaut — Ken Geering

(*'Man is a god who is afraid'*: *Philosopher.*)

Planets far off and sun-blue
beckoned.
He went, and pattered down
the valleyed
clearways of the void.

Questions queued at Mach-zero
Spilling at the cup
of an empty top;

—few answered still:
'have faith, and kneel'

—on neutron cushions?—

till a then-day cosmos-ranged needle
injected hypotheses
unquickly covered and
untheologically sound—

'unthink, and start all over—
—it's World that makes the love go round!'

Copyright

Dear God, by D. W. K. Cotton. Copyright © D. W. K. Cotton 1965.
In Event of Emergency, Call Me, by Malcolm F. Cox. Copyright © Malcolm F. Cox 1968.
Absolute Despair, by James Dempsey. Copyright © James Dempsey 1967.
The Best Butter, by Ian Duplessis. Copyright © Ian Duplessis 1967.
Free Gift?, by Gerald England. Copyright © Gerald England 1968.
Observation 3, by B. Owen Fairbairn. Copyright © B. Owen Fairbairn 1968.
th mouth of my sunday suit, by Robert Fearnley. Copyright © Robert Fearnley 1967.
Paras, by E. G. Firth. Copyright © E. G. Firth 1964.
Slug, by F. W. Flemen. Copyright © F. W Flemen 1967.
Marvels and To My Dog, both by Everard Flintoff. Copyright © Everard Flintoff 1965, 1967.
Fire Power, by Connie Ford. Copyright © Connie Ford 1967.
Sunday Papers, by Cynthia Fuller. Copyright © Cynthia Fuller 1968.
Cosmonaut, by Ken Geering. Copyright © Ken Geering 1964.
Hooked, by Olga Gibb. Copyright © Olga Gibb 1967.
Out Of This Cave, by M. Munro Gibson. Copyright © M. Munro Gibson 1967.
Neutrality, by John Gilham. Copyright © John Gilham 1967.
Teach-In, and Mohandas Gandhi and the Onion Pickers, both by David Gill. Copyright © David Gill 1962, 1967.
Aynshunt Ayelind: Summer 1965, by Mike Golding. Copyright © Mike Golding 1965.
After School, by J. D. Goodger. Copyright © J. D. Goodger 1966.
Night-Walk, by David Goulding. Copyright © David Goulding 1967.
Supremacy, by R. G. Gregory. Copyright © R. G. Gregory 1968.
Petronella, by Jeffrey Grenfell-Hill. Copyright © Jeffrey Grenfell-Hill 1966.
Three Haiku, by Anthony E. Harckham. Copyright © Anthony E. Harckham 1966.
Twentieth Century Hymn, by Mick Hawes. Copyright © Mick Hawes 1968.
An Atheist's Prayer, by Sean Healy. Copyright © Sean Healy 1965.
Memo to a Town Planner, by Richard Herbert. Copyright © Richard Herbert 1968.
Warehouseman, by Lette Heselton. Copyright © Lette Heselton 1968.
Smoke More Pot, by D. M. Hopper. Copyright © D. M. Hopper 1966.
Home, by Norman Humphreys. Copyright © Norman Humphreys 1967.
Frequency 7, by Michael R. Hunt. Copyright © Michael R. Hunt 1967.
The Dam Busters, by Norman Iles. Copyright © Norman Iles 1965.
News, by Norman S. Jackson. Copyright © Norman S. Jackson 1965.

Plot Forgotten and Forgiven, by James Johnson. Copyright © James George Johnson 1968.
Road Signs, by Dilys Henrik Jones. Copyright © Dilys Henrik Jones 1964.
Weeding, by Joan Jordan. Copyright © Joan Jordan 1966.
The March of the Gods, by M. L. Jordan. Copyright © M. L. Jordan 1967.
A Surrealist Painting by Bill Crook, by Peter Jury. Copyright © Peter Jury 1964.
Silence, by Margaret Kenmore. Copyright © Margaret Kenmore 1965.
Hand Out the Song Sheets, Dora's Climbed Another Mountain, by David Kernek. Copyright © David Kernek 1967.
Spring Etc and Rains Come, both by Ronald Kerr. Copyright © Ronald Kerr 1967.
Requiem for Ann and Elegy for Taffy, both by Pete King. Copyright © Pete King 1968.
Time, by Terry Kingham. Copyright © Terry Kingham 1966.
Ebb Tide, by Margo Laird. Copyright © Margo Laird 1965.
In the Still Summer Heat, by A. C. Landor. Copyright © A. C. Landor 1966.
The Ballad of Malcolm X, by Robert Leach. Copyright © Robert Leach 1967.
Dead Beat, by David J. Lee. Copyright © David J. Lee 1966.
History, Geography and Anarchy, by Ian Lennon. Copyright © Ian Lennon 1967.
Piccadilly Tube Station, by William Limmer. Copyright © William Limmer 1966.
Sutherland, by Alfred McClintock. Copyright © Alfred McClintock 1966.
Newsflash, by Helen MacGowan. Copyright © Helen MacGowan 1968.
Rodin's Bronze 'L'Homme au Nez Cassé', by N. G. Maroudas. Copyright © N. G. Maroudas 1965.
Primitive and In Towns Men Come Together, both by Patricia Martland. Copyright © Patricia Martland 1963, 1968.
Eleven Lines In Prayer, by Derek May. Copyright © Derek May 1968.
Barbarella and Mandelbaum, both by David Mycroft. Copyright © David Mycroft 1965, 1967.
For Sweet-Dee, by Michael Parker. Copyright © Michael Parker 1964.
An Offer and Conscience, both by R. L. Parsley. Copyright © R. L. Parsley 1968.
Public Service 1966, by Molly Partis. Copyright © Molly Partis 1966.
Man of Steel, by Allan Peel. Copyright © Allan Peel 1967.
Miss Pike and Miss Minnow, by Juanita Peirse. This poem is copyright. All rights are reserved by the author.

Don Mario Borelli's Family, by Margaret Perkins. Copyright © Margaret Perkins 1968.
The Man in Bradford and Clock, both by Robert J. Pickles. Copyright © R. J. Pickles 1963.
Man in Orbit and For Samuel B......, both by D. O. Pitches. Copyright © D. O. Pitches 1967.
Poppy Day Contradictions and Cain, both by Jacqueline Pointer. Copyright © Jacqueline Pointer 1967.
A Day, Analogue, and Stones, all by John Porter. Copyright © John Porter 1966, 1968.
Poisoned Sea, by Brian S. Pratt. Copyright © Brian S. Pratt 1968.
Extol the Unregarded Men, by W. S. Rainbird. Copyright © W. Stewart Rainbird 1967.
Stage One, by M. W. Ramsden. Copyright © M. W. Ramsden 1966.
The Real Thing, and White is the Colour of My Dying Frame, both by Tony Rand. Copyright © Tony Rand 1967, 1968.
Love, by C. J. Randall. Copyright © Christopher J. Randall 1968.
Dead End And Not Coming Back and Synthesis, both by Timothy Read. Copyright © Timothy Read 1966, 1967.
The Bronze Horseman, by Louise J. Rosenberg. Copyright © Louise J. Rosenberg 1967.
A Good Year and Consideration, both by Stan Rounds. Copyright © Stanley Rounds 1967.
Sennen, by Christina Savage. Copyright © Christina Savage 1967.
On Holiday, by Grahame Smith. Copyright © Grahame Smith 1967.
A Truth?, by Peter T. Smith. Copyright © Peter T. Smith 1968.
On the T.V. Report of the Opening of the Ku Klux Klan in Britain and A Thinker, both by Robert Smith. Copyright © Robert Smith 1968.
Silhouette Girl, by David Staniland. Copyright © David Staniland 1966.
Winter, by Simon Stelfox. This poem is copyright. All rights are reserved by the author.
Object and Subject, by Jennett T. Stewart. Copyright © Jennett T. Stewart 1965.
Three Japanese Fishermen, by Terence Strachan. Copyright © Terence Strachan 1965.
Rearguard Action, by John L. Street. Copyright © John L. Street 1968.
1946, by Elizabeth Stuttard. Copyright © Elizabeth Stuttard 1966.
Thoughts, by Brian Dormer Taylor. Copyright © Brian Dormer Taylor 1967.
Stupid, by Graham Thomas. Copyright © Graham Thomas 1968.
Witch-Hunt, by Harry Thomas. Copyright © Harry Thomas 1968.
2 Up Left, by Anne Thomson. Copyright © Anne Thomson 1968.

Sic Transit, by Cartwright Timms. Copyright © Cartwright Timms 1968.

From a Railway Carriage, by Harry Tomlinson. Copyright © Harry Tomlinson 1967.

Equation, by R. J. Tucker. Copyright © Rob J. Tucker 1966.

No Grey Days, by Judy Upton-Kemp. Copyright © Judy Upton-Kemp 1966.

A Lifetime of Scrawled Obscenities, by David Weale. Copyright © David Weale 1968.

Poem, by Asoka Weerasinghe. Copyright © Asoka Weerasinghe 1967.

Dreams, by Peter Whitehead. Copyright © Peter Whitehead 1965.

Credo, by Anthony Whittaker. Copyright © Anthony Whittaker 1966.

Au Bord de l'Eau, by Maurice Wilkins. Copyright © Maurice Wilkins 1960.

British Chivalry, by Eric A. Willats. Copyright © Eric A. Willats 1968.

Timid in the Rain, by Malcolm Woolridge. Copyright © Malcolm Woolridge 1967.

Acknowledgements

All the poems in *It's World That Makes The Love Go Round* have previously appeared in *Breakthru* International Poetry Magazine, and some also in *Breakthru* Publications: *Love Poetry*, *Nature Poetry*, *Poetry for Peace*, *Poetry from the People*, *Poetry for the Left*, and *Poetry for the City & Machine Age*. The following poems have also been published elsewhere:

Time Stands Still, by Keith Armstrong. Previously published in *Circle Books* by Keith Armstrong, 1968.

Vocation, by James Barbour. Previously published in *The Glasgow Herald.*

Common Names, by Gillian Bence-Jones. Previously published in *Scrip Poetry Magazine.*

To Muhammad Ali, by Arthur Charles. Previously published by Arthur Charles 1967.

Primitive, by Patricia Martland. Previously published in *Outposts Publications* (London) 1966.

Miss Pike and Miss Minnow, by Juanita Peirse. Previously published by The Hand and Flower Press (Aldington, Kent), 1952.

Stage One, by M. W. Ramsden. Previously published in *Order and Chaos* by M. W. Ramsden (*Outposts Publications*, London, 1966).

On Holiday, by Grahame Smith. Previously published in *Track*, 1967.

Silhouette Girl, by David Staniland. Previously published in *Space* (House Journal to the Benn Group of Publishers), 1966.

1946, by Elizabeth Stuttard: permission to quote from *Snow in Europe*, by David Gascoyne, kindly given by André Deutsch Ltd.

Au Bord de l'Eau, by Maurice Wilkins. Previously published in *The Seeker*, by Maurice Wilkins (The Dolmen Press, Dublin, 1960).

Contents

HATE

PROTEST

CITY & MACHINE AGE

PEACE & WAR